For Me and My House

By Tom Harmon

For Me and My House

ISBN: 978-1-60920-030-5
Printed in the United States of America

Cover photo by Steve McCormick
Back cover photo by Steve McCormick
Edited by Bob English
Proofed by Mary Evenson

Library of Congress Cataloging-in-Publication Data

API
Ajoyin Publishing, Inc.
P.O. 342
Three Rivers, MI 49093
www.ajoyin.com

Please direct your inquiries to admin@ajoyin.com

Contents

FOREWORD

Writing a book on the family is risky business at best. It can be easily misinterpreted that the one writing the book is an authority on solving all the issues that face marriage and family. The simple truth is that our marriage and family has turned out better than we could have hoped. We give all the glory to God, but quite honestly we are still trying to figure out some of the things we did right. We recall all too quickly the many things we did wrong. All the same, this book is very dear to my heart and the one I have most wanted to write. Writing this book has been as much a joint effort as building our family. So much of what we view as success could never have occurred without Joyce, her sensitivity to the Lord's grace in her life and toward me, our children and grandchildren.

One thing we know that was right is that together we sought the Lord on how to have a marriage that would glorify Him. Together we sought His guidance on how to raise godly children, how to bless them and pray for them. As our children have grown up, married and are building families of their own, together we are seeking the Lord about our role as godly grandparents. We have learned that parenting and grand parenting is easy, *good* parenting and grand parenting is a little more difficult, and *godly* parenting and grand parenting is impossible without a relationship with God.

This book will include some of the scriptural reasons why we do some of the things we do as a family, why we place such a high priority on our marriage and children, why we have a yearly family consecration and, just what *is* a family consecration. I might quickly add that we do not have a perfect marriage nor family but God has surely blessed our feeble efforts to honor Him. We hope this book will be an encouragement to our children as well as to any who may be seeking some direction of faith in their own family. Both Joyce and I feel that leaving a legacy of faith is the only inheritance of lasting value.

Preface

The most basic human relationships are found in the family. Few things affect us more in our development towards adulthood than the kind of family we were raised in. Families shape individuals. Individuals shape families. Families shape nations. Nations shape the world. It is hard for a nation to rise above the caliber of family found in it. Most people would agree that family is important and even more would agree that they desire a good family. But who is the authority on the family and what instructions, if any, are there?

I often refer to the Bible as a family album. It begins with the story of Adam and Eve and their marriage. It continues on with the story of their children and their marriages, as well as their grandchildren and their marriages. This biblical record of their journey is relevant for us today. How they faced the trials of life in a fallen world haven't changed much since the beginning of time. Therefore, this family album will be the major resource for the contents of this book. If we can learn some basics that never change, God will custom design a family that will glorify Him. In glorifying Him we receive the most good.

CHAPTER ONE

Understanding the First Family

The Creator designed marriage and the family. "And Adam said, This is now bone of my bones, and flesh of my flesh; she shall be called Woman, because she was taken out of man. Therefore shall a man leave his father and his mother, and shall cleave unto his wife; and they shall be one flesh" (Gen. 2:23–24). They were created without sin and lived in perfect fellowship. "And they were both naked, the man and his wife, and were not ashamed" (Gen. 2:25). If ever there was a time on the earth when things were perfect, it was then. They had the perfect marriage, the perfect home, the perfect life. How could this perfect home and marriage completely unravel? What happened that brought about the loss of their joy and the destruction of their paradise? Could what happened in the first family possibly be behind our problems today?

A God-Made Man

There are those who believe the theory that the origin of man developed through an evolutionary process over millions of years. In many areas of the world this is taught as a scientific fact. Those who believe this to be true have a great deal of faith, much more than I am capable of. I believe man was made by God from the dust of the ground, then given breath by His Spirit and man became a living soul. "And the Lord God formed man of the dust of the ground, and breathed into his nostrils the breath of life; and man became a living soul" (Gen.2:7). "Know ye that the Lord, he is God; it is he who hath made us, and not we ourselves; we are his people and the sheep of his pasture" (Ps.100:3).

The first occupation of man was to be a farmer. He was to till the soil, keep it and help it produce. "And the Lord God took the man, and put him into the Garden of Eden, to till it and to keep it" (Gen 2:15).

A Farmer at Heart

The only thing I ever really wanted to do with my life was to be a farmer. I wanted to marry, have children and live and work on a farm; more specifically a dairy farm. As a child I would spend time each summer with my grandparents on their dairy farm. I fell in love with the sights and sounds and even the fragrances of the barn and fields. I spent hours, especially during my teens and twenties, dreaming of some day becoming a dairy farmer.

I have always loved to garden and we've had one ever since we lived in our first house. I grew up around good gardeners; my grandparents, parents, aunts and uncles all planted and harvested various kinds of fruits, berries and vegetables. There is a special sense of accomplishment that comes from eating food you have planted and cared for. It even seems to taste better when you've had a hand in it. We are always careful not to say that we grow things in our garden, but rather that we plant things in our garden, God grows them. We can fertilize and till the soil. We can plant the seeds and even keep it watered and weeded, but we certainly can't make things grow. It is God who gives the increase.

That One Forbidden Tree

God made man in His likeness but not in His exactness. God is from everlasting to everlasting, self-existent, self-sufficient, omniscient, omnipotent and omnipresent. Man is not! Man was created with needs. God needs nothing. "God who made the world and all things in it, seeing that he is Lord of heaven and earth, dwelleth not in temples made with hands, neither is worshiped with men's hands, as though he needed any thing, seeing he giveth to all life, and breath and all things" (Acts 17:24–25). God doesn't need government. Man needs government. God established government for man when He placed a tree in the middle of the Garden of Eden and commanded him not to eat of it. This tree was called "the tree of the knowledge of good and evil." God made it clear to Adam not to eat of this tree for if he did, that very day he would die. It was right for this knowledge to be placed in the garden. If not, God wouldn't have placed it there. I believe the tree was called the knowledge of "good and evil" because evil is never more dangerous than when camouflaged in something that looks good. When a man fills his life with many good works it becomes difficult for him to see the evil that lives within the dim regions of his sinful heart. That sin was not in Adam's heart as it is in ours. No, the knowledge of evil that comes from sin was in the fruit of the forbidden tree. If Adam were to eat the fruit the fruit would be inside him. As everything you eat ends up inside of you, the knowledge of evil and sin would be inside Adam.

The fruit from all the other trees produced life but the fruit of this tree would produce death. As always, God spoke the truth. Man would have been better off if he would have believed God's words.

It's Not Good for Man to Be Alone

As God finished creating things He always said it was good. The creation of man was also good, but it wasn't good that he should be alone. So God put Adam into a deep sleep and performed the first surgery. God took a rib from Adam, made a woman and presented her to him. She was to be a helper and completer of the man. Together they would have a greater capacity to fulfill God's design than either of them could alone. She was equal in all her creation to reflect the glory and goodness of God. She was behind in nothing except perhaps physical strength. She was fully aware of the government of God and her responsibility to obey. She knew the command concerning the tree of the knowledge of good and evil, as evidenced by her response to the serpent. We do well to understand as much as we can about what comes next.

The Tempter

There is a real devil who is also called Satan. He is the enemy of God and hates everything that is holy. He is a liar and the father of lies. He is a murderer and a thief. He is the spirit that works in the sons of disobedience. He is wicked, merciless and cruel. When Satan tried to usurp the throne of God, he was cast out of heaven (see Isa. 14:12–15). God had given man authority over all creation and Satan was bent on stealing that authority from Adam. Satan was hoping God would cast man out away from His presence as He had him. What happened to the first family next has had ramifications that have affected every family throughout time and will, even into eternity. First, Satan attempted to convince man to doubt God's Word, then he flat out called God a liar and lastly he promised them independence from authority. Let's pick up the narrative in Genesis, chapter 3: "Now the serpent was more subtle than any beast of the field which the Lord God had made, and he said to the woman, Yea, hath God said, ye shall not eat of every tree of the garden? And the woman said unto the serpent, We may eat of the fruit of the trees of the garden; but of the fruit of the tree which is in the midst of the garden, God hath said, Ye shall not eat of it, neither shall ye touch it, lest ye die. And the serpent said unto the woman, Ye shall not surely die; for God doth know that in the day ye eat thereof, then your eyes shall be opened, and ye shall be as God, knowing good and evil. And when the woman saw that the tree was good for food, and that it was pleasant to the eyes, and a tree to be desired to make one wise, she took the fruit thereof, and did eat, and gave also unto her husband with her; and he did eat" (Gen. 3:1–6).

Death

God had made it clear that in the day they ate of the tree they would surely die, and die they did. They died spiritually. They no longer had fellowship with God in the spirit. Their oneness with God was gone. They were still alive in their body and soul. They had a functioning mind. They could exercise their will. They could feel emotion. They could even run and try to hide themselves, but they were spiritually dead. God could no more have fellowship with them than a man could have fellowship with a deceased wife laying in a coffin. One obvious thing about a dead person is that they do not respond to live people.

If they do respond, they are not dead. The first man and woman were now dead in their trespasses and sin. They would forever pass on that spiritual death to their offspring. Man from then on was born physically, mentally, emotionally alive, but spiritually dead.

Man's New Nature

The very moment they had eaten the forbidden fruit a radical change occurred. They looked at each other with shame and regret. A fear came over them that they had not known before. They used to look forward to God coming in the cool of the day to walk and talk together. Now, the only thing they wanted to do was hide from Him. Nothing says it better than the Scriptures. "And the eyes of them both were opened, and they knew that they were naked; and they sewed fig leaves together, and made themselves aprons. And they heard the voice of the Lord God walking in the garden in the cool of the day; and Adam and his wife hid themselves from the presence of the Lord God among the trees of the garden" (Gen. 3:7–8). I am sure Satan was just waiting for God to cast them out of His presence, but what he saw was certainly not what he expected. The omniscient God of the universe reached down to man in love through a series of questions that ultimately led Adam to repentance and restored fellowship. Things were tense as God revealed their new nature to them. They didn't like what they saw. If it weren't for God's intervention they wouldn't have had a clue where to turn or what to do.

Where Are You

"And the Lord God called unto Adam, and said unto him, Where art thou?" (Gen.3:9). God didn't ask Adam where he had been or where he was going; he asked him where he was. The sin nature of man seems to always want to live either in the past or the future, rarely in the present. Because of sin, man often doesn't know where he is. He knows better where he's been or where he hopes to go, but rarely does he know where he is. By the way, do you think the all-knowing God knew where Adam was? God wasn't perplexed. He knew what had happened to Adam and Eve. If there is anyone who knows where we are, at any given moment of life, it is God. If any man truly wants to know his present condition, he will have to bring God into the mix. If he does not, he must be content to live life never really knowing where he is. So then why did God ask them where they were? God asked because His goodness, to the chagrin of Satan, led the first couple to repentance, forgiveness and restored fellowship. This repentance, forgiveness and restored fellowship can never come to pass unless we first know where we are. This point cannot be emphasized enough. If you don't know where you are, you are lost.

Hearing Voices

Adam heard God's voice and was afraid. Adam also heard another voice telling him he was naked. "And [Adam] said, I heard thy voice in the garden, and I was afraid, because I was naked; and I hid myself. And [God] said, who told thee thou wast naked?" (Gen.3:10–11a). After their failure to obey God, I'm sure the accuser of the brethren lost no time in reminding Adam of God's very Word: "in the day you eat of the forbidden fruit you will surely die." No doubt Satan told him he was naked and should try and hide himself; maybe disguise himself with some camouflage-colored aprons. Just blend in with the rest of the surroundings and God will never know.

When Satan successfully tempts us, he loves to torment us with our failure, telling us to run farther from God. Satan knew God's mercy. God had not instantly bound him and cast him into the lake of fire. Satan seems to be in a panic, hoping man would not be given the chance to respond to God's mercy. After they ate of the fruit, evil must have come in like a flood on Adam and Eve. But the patience and longsuffering of God prevailed.

The Shocking Nature of Sin

God continued with His fellowship-restoring line of questioning. "Hast thou eaten of the tree, whereof I commanded thee that thou shouldest not eat?" (Gen 3:11b) Adam is the one being asked, not Eve. This is the big question and his answer revealed much about the troubles that have plagued him and his descendants ever since. What he said shows the depths of depravity to which his sin has affected us all. "And the man said, the woman **whom thou gavest me**, she gave me of the tree and I did eat" (Gen. 3:12 emphasis mine). The shocking nature of sin is that it never accepts any responsibility for its actions but instead blames somebody else. First, Adam blamed the woman then immediately turns the focus against God for presenting her to him. It's as if he censures God for causing his rebellion. Can you hear Adam reflecting? "I was getting along just fine before she came along. I never asked for her. It was Your idea to take my rib and make her. None of this would ever have happened if You hadn't thought I needed a wife. Why did You ever allow Satan in here in the first place? If I had been designing things, none of this would have ever happened. Why did You put that stinking tree in the garden? I would have put it off in some obscure corner where no one would have ever seen it. And another thing: if You knew the fruit was dangerous why did You make it look so delicious? Yes, if I had been calling the shots everything in the garden would still be perfect."

Man instantly became self-righteous, self-centered and arrogantly self-absorbed. Satan had told them they would be like God, knowing good and evil. They now believed that they had become the captain of their own ship, the master of their own destiny. They could look at life and evaluate what was best for them. They wouldn't need God telling them what to do and what not to do. Man's fellowship with God was gone and his prideful new nature thought he could get along just fine without Him. "Professing themselves to be wise, they became fools, and changed the glory of the incorruptible God into an image made like to corruptible man…" (Rom. 1:22–23a). Oh, into what unimaginable abyss of depravity had he fallen? Little did he know of the horrors that would come upon him and his descendants because of this sin. The worst horror of all: his children would come out of the womb with a sin nature. "Behold I was shaped in iniquity, and in sin did my mother conceive me" (Ps.51:5).

Blameshifting Continues

"And the Lord God said unto the woman, What is this that thou hast done? And the woman said, The serpent beguiled me, and I did eat" (Gen. 3:13). Her response was the same as her husband's. She also had the same sinful nature as her husband. She accurately blamed Satan for the temptation but she also blamed God as though He had left her powerless to resist the temptation. Had He? "There hath no temptation taken you but such as is common to man; but God is faithful, who will not allow you to be tempted above what you are able; but will with the temptation also make a way of escape, that you may be able to bear it" (1 Cor. 10:13). That scripture was just as true in the garden as it is today. You may ask, what was her way of escape? How could she have resisted the tempter? Don't forget she had been given the Word of God: "don't eat of the tree or you will die." If she had stood firm on that truth and quoted it each and every time the tempter lied to her, she would have escaped. If Adam and Eve had quoted it together, they wouldn't have sinned. When Satan tempted Jesus in the wilderness, each time He said: "It is written... It is written... It is written..." Jesus the Incarnate Word Himself quoted Scripture. Satan is no match for the power of God's Word. If Eve would have stood firm on the truth of God's Word she would have defeated the enemy of her soul and made him flee from the garden. Satan had lied to Eve. But is being lied to the same as being deceived? No, you are only deceived when you know the truth and yet chose to believe the lie. Eve was deceived, but not Adam. "And Adam was not deceived, but the woman" (1 Tim. 2:14a). Eve, hearing the lies of the serpent, chose to believe them over the Word of God. When she ate of the fruit of the forbidden tree, instantly she changed. Her glory was gone and Adam knew right well she had sinned. When she presented the fruit to him, he also made a conscious choice. His choice was not a choice to believe the lies however. His choice was to continue a relationship with a woman he could see as opposed to the Spirit of God he could not see. They had never seen God but had been content to walk by faith. God loves faith and desires that we walk by faith and not by sight. We know that without faith it is impossible to please Him. The apostle Paul didn't fear many things but he did fear Satanic lies. Because of sin man is more vulnerable towards believing a lie than believing truth. "But I fear, lest by any means, as the serpent beguiled Eve through his craftiness, so your minds should be corrupted from the simplicity that is in Christ" (2 Cor.11:3). All the more reason to know the truth well, choose to believe it and walk by faith.

The Double Curse

"And the Lord God said unto the serpent, Because thou hast done this, thou art cursed above all cattle, and above every beast of the field; upon thy belly shalt thou go, and dust shalt thou eat all the days of thy life" (Gen. 3:14). God first cursed Satan when He cast him out of heaven for trying to exalt his throne above the stars of God, (Isa. 14:12–15). God cursed him again in the garden after he had usurped all that God had given to man. Satan is now bound for hell, his final doom sealed; he is under a double curse. "And the devil that deceived them was cast into the lake of fire and brimstone, where the beast and the false prophet are, and shall be tormented day and night forever" (Rev. 20:10).

Man is also born under a curse: the curse of the law. The law of God demands perfection. Ask Adam—only one bite of one piece of fruit. If man dies under the curse of the law he also comes under the double curse resulting in the same judgment as Satan. "Then shall he say also to them on the left hand, Depart from me, ye cursed into everlasting fire, prepared for the devil and his angels" (Matt. 25:41).

The Promise

As a result of disobedience sin permeated Adam's body even to the very genetics of his seed, but God made a difference between his seed and the woman's seed. From her seed God promised that one day would come a champion that would crush

Satan's head, receiving only a bruise to His own heel. There was a lot Adam didn't understand, but God's promise gave him hope. This hope enabled him to bear the further consequences of their sin. God spoke to them of the sorrow for his wife in childbearing. He told them of the inevitable power struggles that would come between them. Even the ground would be cursed as a constant reminder of what it could have been. The joy of gardening would change to sorrow as thorns and thistles would relentlessly compete for the nutrients originally designed for the crops. Finally, God told them the news that their bodies, would eventually die and return to the dust from which they came. God's promise was accompanied by that godly commodity called grace. By grace they accepted the consequences of their sin and by faith they believed the promise.

Redemption

When they ate of the fruit of the tree of the knowledge of good and evil, they died. They were spiritually dead to God. But by the mercy and grace of God He led them to repentance. They had no hope of renewed spiritual life except through the promise of God, the promise that God would send life through the seed of the woman. They believed the promise that even after they died and their bodies returned to dust, they would once again be with God. As an expression of Adam's faith he changed the name of his wife from "woman" to "Eve," which means the mother of all living.

Then God in His mercy made coats for them to cover their nakedness. These coats were more than coverings for their bodies, they were evidence that God through a blood sacrifice had forgiven their sins and restored fellowship. God had brought them to life again. The coats of skins, His gift, would surround them as a reminder of His grace. Yes, God drove them out of the garden and they bore the consequences of their sin. But regardless of the difficulties, God had made a provision for their sin: He had redeemed them through the blood of His sacrifice.

Today we understand the fulfillment of God's promise to Adam in the person of God's Son, the Lord Jesus. By grace we understand that we are born sinners who need to be born again. Even so, after we are born again, we still need to deal with indwelling sin, death, temptations and a world that is so obviously not Eden. Understanding the first family is a great beginning in understanding our own families.

CHAPTER TWO

The Purpose of Marriage

Joyce and I were high school sweethearts. We met in the middle of our junior year. As we began to fall in love our thoughts naturally drifted towards marriage. Neither of us had a clue as to the purpose of marriage. Even after we had been married ten years and had four children, I'm not sure we could have given a clear statement as to the purpose of marriage. As I look back now, I probably got married because I thought we would make a good couple. After all, I was in love with me and thought she was too! In all seriousness, I knew very little about this divine institution that God had designed and sanctioned for His glory. All I knew was that I had strong feelings for Joyce and she had them for me. We enjoyed being together and shared many of the same interests. Understanding the purpose of marriage would eventually come. Oh, how we thank God that it did.

Would You Marry Me?

In the late sixties, the popular path traveled if you were getting serious about a girl was to give her a pearl ring. It was kind of a preliminary to an engagement ring, nothing final, but it kind of let people know that you were getting serious. I gave her the pearl ring for Christmas our senior year of high school. The following fall I attended a college 400 miles away while Joyce went to beauty school in Lansing. When I came home for Thanksgiving break I asked her if she would marry me. She said she would love to but I would have to ask her father. She told her folks and the evening was chosen when I would ask her dad. Nervously I asked for her hand in marriage. Her father gave me three things he wanted me to agree to before he would say yes. I was to promise to

#1 Always love her and be faithful to her.
#2 Never harm her in any way.
#3 Allow her to graduate from beauty school before we could get married. That way, she would have some means of support if anything ever happened to me.

Joyce graduated six months later. Two weeks after her graduation we were married.

Marriage Conference

In the fall of 1978, I committed my life to Christ. I was beginning to grow in the Lord and desired to know what He wanted for my life. In the spring of 1980, our church held a marriage conference. The speaker was Craig Massey. He was humorous, yet gave very clear instructions from the Bible on what a marriage and family should look like. Both Joyce and I were convicted and inspired to make some changes. The main thing we took away from the conference was a clear-cut purpose for our marriage. We realized that we had been married for almost ten years and didn't have a purpose.

We chose our purpose statement from Philippians 2:1–4 and have stuck with it ever since. "If there be therefore any consolation in Christ, if any comfort of love, if any FELLOWSHIP OF THE SPIRIT, if any tender mercies and compassions, fulfill ye my joy, that ye be like-minded, having the same love, being of one accord, of one mind. Let nothing be done through strife or vainglory; but in lowliness of mind let each esteem others better than themselves. Look not every man on his own things, but every man also on the things of others" (Phil. 2:1–4, emphasis mine). That was it. The purpose for our marriage would be "Fellowship in the Spirit." The word "fellowship" comes from the Greek word *koinonia* which means oneness. Joyce and I were made one flesh by our covenant before God at our wedding ceremony and consummated those vows on our honeymoon. Both of us were born again and therefore had the capacity to be one in the Spirit. It is impossible to be one in the Spirit if one mate is saved and the other lost. It is as hopeless for an unequally married couple to have fellowship in the Spirit as it would be for a living person to have fellowship with a dead one. They may be able to have a relatively good marriage and love their children and each other, but they could never move into the caliber of oneness that God intended them to share in the Spirit.

Fellowship Explained

God has a relationship with every man, even the atheist, whether he wants one or not. God created him, gave him life and sustains his life. One day that man will stand before his Creator and give an account of his life. "So then every one of us shall give account of himself to God" (Rom 14:12). But even though God has a relationship with every man it does not mean that every man has a relationship with God. "God is a Spirit; and they that worship him must worship him in spirit and in truth" (Jn. 4:24). Man is born spiritually dead, unable to have a relationship with the Spirit of God. However, once a person is born of the Spirit of God he is given a new and living relationship in which he can now experience fellowship with God in the Spirit. "And you hath he made alive who were dead in trespasses and sins" (Eph. 2:1). "That which is born of the flesh is flesh; and that which is born of the Spirit is spirit. Marvel not that I said unto thee, Ye must be born again" (Jn.3:6–7). When God draws a man to Himself by revealing the issue of his sin, that man by grace through faith can confess his sin and receive forgiveness. With such a confession God places His Spirit within him. He raises his dead spirit to life where he is able to have fellowship or oneness with God. This new and eternal relationship with God will never change. Jesus said, "No man can come to me, except the Father, who hath sent me, draw him" (Jn. 6:44a). "For by grace are ye saved through faith; and that not of yourselves, it is gift of God" (Eph. 2:8). "For he that is joined unto the Lord is one spirit" (1 Cor. 6:17). When the truth of Jesus' sacrificial death is embraced by faith that person becomes a new and living creation. "Therefore if any man be in Christ, he is a new creation; old things are passed away; behold all things are become new" (2 Cor. 5:17). We still live in a fallen world. We still have all the same potential of the old man. We still struggle with the old way of living. But all the while, we have a new relationship with God called "fellowship in the Spirit."

Fellowship Desired

The one thing that breaks fellowship between the Christian and God is sin. The one thing that breaks fellowship between a husband and wife is sin, or with any other Christian for that matter. Joyce and I knew what it was like to have sin come between us and break our fellowship. As we grew together, we determined that when this happened we would hold hands and pray. We would ask for forgiveness from God and each other. We made a commitment to humble ourselves before God and each other, to ask Him to bring us back into oneness. We didn't want to let sin build up and come between us. We wanted our love for God to be obvious in how we loved each other. Oneness seemed the best way to do this.

Who's to Blame

When Joyce and I are in fellowship with each other, we know it. When we are out of fellowship with each other, we know it. We have little ways of letting each other know when one of us has offended or failed the other. We all sense when fellowship is broken, but mates have a special sensitivity between themselves. Mates can tell in a look (or the lack of a look), the tone of voice or that withdrawing don't-touch-me kind of body language. When our fellowship is broken, the sin that is in me wants to blame her and the sin that is in her wants to blame me. What a revelation it was when we realized that it wasn't her, and it wasn't me; it was the sin that was in us that was the problem. We loved each other and wanted to do right by each other. The age-old struggle within ourselves is best recorded in Paul's letter to the Romans. "For the good that I would I do not; but the evil which I would not, that I do. Now if I do that I would not, it is no more I that do it, but sin that dwelleth in me. I find then a law that, when I would do good, evil is present with me. For I delight in the law of God after the inward man; but I see another law in my members, warring against the law of my mind, and bringing me into captivity to the law of sin which is in my members. Oh wretched man that I am! Who shall deliver me from the body of this death? I thank God through Jesus Christ our Lord. So then with the mind I myself serve the law of God; but with the flesh the law of sin" (Rom. 7:19–25).

Identifying the Problem

Once you identify the problem you can deal with it. Our problem is indwelling sin. It is that sin we received from our parents, who received it from theirs. It can be traced all the way back to the first family. Praise the Lord, He has made a way of dealing with indwelling sin. The Lord Jesus Christ died for our sins; not only to pay the penalty but also to break the power of sin through the power of His grace. "For sin shall not have dominion over you; for ye are not under the law, but under grace" (Rom. 6:14). As Christians we are going to sin. We don't want to, but the old man still shows the nature of sin which continues to live in our flesh. Just because a person is born again doesn't mean he is going to bat a thousand every time he is tempted. The world we live in is constantly bombarding our minds with a philosophy that is contrary to the ways of God. The devil himself continues to speak his lies. He doesn't know any other language. Without any help from the world or the devil, my own heart is fully capable of the most horrible depravity. "The heart is deceitful above all things, and desperately wicked; who can know it?" (Jer. 17:9).

Problem Solving

Joyce and I memorized and claimed the truths in 1 John 1:5–10. These verses are too good to leave out, so here we go: "This then is the message which we have heard of him, and declare unto you, that God is light, and in him is no darkness at all. If we say we have fellowship with him, and walk in darkness, we lie, and do not the truth; But if we walk in the light, as he is in the light, we have fellowship one with another, and the blood of Jesus Christ his Son cleanseth us from all sin. If we say that we have no sin, we deceive ourselves, and the truth is not in us. If we confess our sins, he is faithful and just to forgive us our sins, and to cleanse us from all unrighteousness. If we say we have not sinned, we make him a liar, and his word is not in us."

In this text, light is used metaphorically of the holiness of God. Darkness represents sin. Remember, sin is what breaks fellowship with God and with each other. It is only possible for sinful man to have fellowship with a holy God if he will acknowledge his sin, confess it and repent. Repentance is the act of turning away from our desire to be independent from God. Repentance is turning from sin to God. Confession without repentance is mockery. When the Word says, "If we walk in the light as he is in the light" it is describing the way we live. If we continue to practice our sin with nothing more than a request now and then for cleansing and forgiveness without any intention of turning from our sin we deceive ourselves. Self deception is the worst form of deception because it means we've lied to ourselves for so long we believe it. Joyce and I knew that if the purpose of our marriage was fellowship and oneness we would have to deal with sin. We determined to look squarely at the sin issues in our lives and ask God to help us change. Now we knew what to do and why to do it but the difficult part would be putting it into practice. Academic theology always sounds good in the lecture hall but doesn't always look that great in the lab.

Laboratory Tested

I include the following illustration with some reservation but it is a classic of how this stuff works. Joyce and I had made the commitment to hold hands and pray whenever some sin had broken our fellowship. As we began to practice our commitment, the Lord blessed and we discovered a new level of love and fellowship. The eventual day finally came though when something happened that broke our fellowship. Words were exchanged. Looks were given. I began to have "the pout" on. For the life of me I can't remember what started it but I know I was upset with her for something. Sounds stupid, doesn't it? But many times that is just what sin does. It makes fools of us. I was descending into an "I don't want to be around you" attitude so I went upstairs to our bedroom. I was going to change into my old clothes, go outside and work in the yard. The Holy Spirit was trying to reason with me. He was telling me to humble myself and get this thing right. I remember telling Him it was *her* turn to humble herself and make things right.

My dear wife came upstairs and said, "Honey, let's pray." The ugliness of sin was really coming on and I did not want to pray. She asked me if I would forgive her. I will never forget my response. I had been doing a series of messages on the subject of forgiveness so I said to her, "I guess I have to, the Bible says so." Her shoulders dropped to acknowledge her disappointment with my sinful answer. God is so merciful! If I had been God, I would have toasted me right there.

The Lord gave her grace to say once again, "Honey, let's pray." I knew what she meant. She wanted me to pray, but I didn't want to. She held out her hands and I extended mine. My hands were in the submissive position, palms up. There was about as much life in them as a couple of dead fish. She bowed her head while I just looked at the wall behind her, my blinded eyes wide open. My capacity for depravity was in IMAX© form. I said in an apathetic tone, "You pray." The Lord gave her grace and as she began to pray, she made contact with Deity. Quickly she became broken over her own sinful attitude. Before she had time to finish her short prayer, I was humbled before the Lord and with great shame over my conduct, I confessed and repented of my sinful attitude. During this time my hands changed from sinful hands to loving hands. Before we were through praying, we were in each other arms in deeper fellowship than we had known before. This happened about thirty years ago and I wish I could say that we have never had anything come between us since but the simple truth is we have had to repeat that same process on a number of occasions. Today, Joyce and I enjoy perfect fellowship over 95 percent of the time. When sin shows its ugly head, we have a proven solution to the problem: it's the Word of God. Laboratory tested and proven successful.

Consider the Cost

You may say that humbling yourself is too high a price to pay to have fellowship. May I lovingly say that the cost of pride and broken fellowship is much higher? Pride may lead your marriage to a place you never dreamed it would go. It is risky to live out of fellowship. You leave yourself vulnerable to all kinds of temptations that otherwise could have been avoided. The devil licks his lips and knows it won't be long until pampered pride will make him a meal. "Humble yourself in the sight of the Lord, and he shall lift you up" (Jas. 4:10). "And be clothed with humility; for God resisteth the proud, and giveth grace to the humble" (1 Pet. 5:5c). The humble man may have Satan to oppose him but the proud man is in a much worse fix. God Almighty resists the proud but giveth grace to the humble. The Lord Jesus humbled Himself and became obedient unto death, even the death of the cross. He did that to break the power of sin and make it possible for us to have a new and living relationship with Him, a relationship of fellowship in the Spirit. His example is one well worth following. Once a person gets a good taste of fellowship in the Spirit, no cost is too high. When one experiences oneness with Deity, nothing less will satisfy.

A Poor Substitute

There is great contagious power in both humility and pride. When either Joyce or I see our sin, we usually try to see who can be first at humility. We try to be the first to get right with God and then each other. Pride only prolongs the inevitable. We know we can't live with something between us. We know we are going to have to make it right sooner or later, so why not sooner? Life is too short and death is too certain to waste any of it being out of fellowship. One of the great dangers of pride and broken fellowship is the temptation to substitute peace for fellowship. Now peace is better than war but it is a poor substitute for fellowship. You learn to exist together but miss out on the life of fellowship you were intended to enjoy. For example, we have peace with Russia, but we don't have fellowship with them. I mean we get along with them but we are not on the same page. The sad truth is that kind of peace is a false peace, a man-made peace and temporary at best. Man-made peace is when you merely tolerate one another. Eventually a tolerant peace deteriorates making it harder and harder to come to humility and reconciliation. It is not the kind of peace that Jesus gives us. "Peace I leave with you, my peace I give unto you; not as the world giveth, give I unto you. Let not your heart be troubled, neither let it be afraid" (Jn. 14:27). Jesus-given peace comes with fellowship in the Spirit. This peace is also called the fruit of the Spirit. It is easily identifiable as a peace that passes all understanding. We know it's impossible to generate this kind of peace in our own power. This kind is signed by the Prince of Peace. Eventually, you come to recognize the signature.

Separation

Though man-made peace can endure for a long time and even look on the outside as though all is well, eventually it descends into separation. You may live in the same house, eat at the same table, sleep in the same bed, but eventually you will realize you are strangers. You may stay together physically but you know in your hearts you have moved apart. It's not that uncommon for people after 25, 35, 45 years of marriage to call it quits and separate. It is wiser to keep your accounts current and deal with things as they come along. Staying in fellowship makes your marriage stronger the older you grow. Compromising with fellowship only makes you more vulnerable as time goes along. Growing old isn't for sissies; mainly because it's the harvest time for what we have sown in our younger years.

Sowing and Reaping

The law of sowing and reaping is a law of life established in the Garden of Eden. It is with us even today. "Be not deceived; God is not mocked; for whatsoever a man soweth, that shall he also reap. For he that soweth to the flesh shall of the flesh reap corruption; but he that soweth to the Spirit shall of the Spirit reap life everlasting. And let us not be weary in well doing; for in due season we shall reap, if we faint not" (Gal. 6:7–9). When we humble ourselves, we are sowing to the Spirit and in due season it will yield God's blessing. Pride is always sowing to the flesh; it always sets us up for a fall. It's also the reason for most of the contention in our lives. "Only by pride cometh contention, but with the well advised is wisdom" (Prov.13:10). Pride always blinds me to seeing my wrong, but gives me 20/20 vision on seeing the faults of others. It's no wonder Jesus told us to deal with the log that's in our own eye before we help the person with the speck in their eye.

A Mercful God

Regardless of where we are in our journey of faith or our marriages, we can know of a certainty that God is merciful, especially to those who reverence Him. "Blessed be the God and Father of our Lord Jesus Christ, who according to his abundant mercy hath begotten us again unto a living hope by the resurrection of Jesus Christ from the dead" (1 Pet.1:3). You may be thinking it's too late to come to the throne of grace and ask for mercy and help from God. David said, "I had fainted, unless I had believed to see the goodness of the Lord in the land of the living" (Psa.27:13). The God Who gives us life has also given us a living hope. If your marriage needs a clearer purpose, choose fellowship. When sin breaks your fellowship with God and each other, humble yourselves hold hands and ask forgiveness of God and each other. Ask Him to restore oneness and it just may be that He will begin to turn your marriage around and restore to you the years the locust have eaten. When fellowship is restored with heaven and home, God is glorified and we marvel at His goodness.

For Me And My House

I had the privilege of performing the wedding ceremonies for all our children. This included our standard marriage counseling. I thoroughly enjoyed our sessions and felt it was profitable for all of us. I encouraged them toward the goal of fellowship in their marriage. I told them the longer they lived in fellowship the less they would like to live without it. How precious it is when husband and wife dwell together in unity. Eventually they would find themselves racing to see who could be first to humble themselves and reconcile their differences. Fellowship with God and with each other is such a glorious way to live life. Their fellowship would have a profound effect on their children and even the mates they would one day marry. Not all may agree with the following advice I gave them. I told them before rushing off to some type of full-time ministry, they would do well to take a decade or so and establish their home. For those who may disagree with this, I can only respond that we must all give an account of ourselves before God. (Rom 14:12). Remember the title of this book is not, "As for Me and Your House," but "As for Me and My House." Part of being godly men is assuming our responsibility to step up to the plate and make the best choices we can make to lead our families in a godly direction. Ministries and ministry styles come and go. Even in the past fifty years the church has gone through a metamorphosis of change in worship, in youth activities, in family integration, in senior outreach, in theological issues and even in its purpose. It seems hard, in my opinion, for the church to ever rise above the caliber of the families that it's made of.

Establish

It takes time for something to become established. Relationships take time to become strong. It takes experience to know how to handle the stress of life. A farmer is usually a better farmer after ten years of farming than when he just started. A combat-hardened soldier is usually a better soldier than one who just finished boot camp. It takes time for Christians to become established in their faith and in their home. "As ye have therefore received Christ Jesus the Lord, so walk ye in him; rooted and built up in him, and established in the faith, as ye have been taught, abounding with thanksgiving" (Col.2:6–7).

You might as well hear it now: all hell will oppose you having a godly marriage and home. But if you will begin casting all your cares upon Him knowing that He cares for you and if you are seriously determined to stand against the devil, in time God will establish you in your home. "Casting all your care upon him; for He careth for you. Be sober, be vigilant, because your adversary the devil, as a roaring lion, walketh about seeking whom he may devour; whom resist steadfast in the faith, knowing that the same afflictions are accomplished in your brethren that are in the world. But the God of all grace, who hath called us unto his eternal glory by Christ Jesus, after that ye have suffered a while, make you perfect, establish, strengthen, settle you" (1 Pet.5:7–10). Becoming established in your walk with the Lord, your marriage, parenting, church, job or anything of value to you will have to travel down this process of time. Choose your priorities, live your life accordingly and you will become established in what you live and believe.

CHAPTER THREE

How To Raise Godly Children

Parenting is easy, good parenting is much more difficult and godly parenting is impossible without God. For the parents who want to raise godly children, they must first decide which god they will serve. There are many gods to choose from in this old world, but for the Christian there is only one true God. He is the one who has revealed Himself to us in the Bible.

There are many principles and guidelines in Scripture which can benefit any home or family during their brief stay on earth, yet never bring a person to the place of godliness. Godly children are those who have a relationship with God. They know who He is and desire to live a life that pleases Him. Just to raise good children and never have them know God seems to have missed the whole point of parenting, yet it has been a common practice since the beginning of time.

What Is Godliness?

Godliness is the piety a man has toward God as well as the conduct of life which springs from a proper relationship with

Him through the gospel. Godliness is not simply believing *in* God, but devotion *toward* God that results from that belief. Religious faith is empty without godliness. “But thou, O man of God, flee these things; and follow after righteousness, godliness, faith, love, patience, meekness. Fight the good fight of faith, lay hold on eternal life, unto which thou art also called, and hast professed a good profession before many witnesses” (1 Tim.6:11–12). Godliness is the sum total and character of one’s faith and virtue. It is not something we do because of some religious obligation or sense of duty alone. Godliness is the reflection of a relationship with God through the indwelling person of Christ.

Reflections

It has been said that the Christian life is more caught than taught. It is easier for the child to learn if the parent is willing to say, “do as I do,” as opposed to, “do as I say.” The simple truth is, most of us follow our parents’ example not their instruction. Children are a reflection of their parents. “As in water face answereth to face, so the heart of man to man” (Prov. 27:19). Children have a way of being the mirror of their parents’ souls. Therefore it would seem like simple logic to ask the question, “if I want my children to know and love God, do I know and love God? If I want them to walk in the ways of the Lord, do I walk in the ways of the Lord?” It would seem reasonable to pursue this manner of questioning about everything from spontaneous obedience to the voice of the Holy Spirit to the things that are established with pen and ink in His holy Word.

Obedience

There are few things that adorn a home with greater beauty than the relationship of a loving parent and an obedient child. The peace of God is upon that home and all who live there enjoy it. Those who visit instantly recognize it. Rebellion and competition are overcome by the simple presence of trust and willing obedience. Submission to authority is seen as a great treasure and worth any cost of self-denial. Is it any wonder the first commandment with promise is "Honor thy father and mother… that it may be well with thee, and thou mayest live long on the earth." (Eph 6:2–3). Well, let's cut to the chase. "Children obey your parents in the Lord; for this is right" (Eph. 6:1). What oftentimes is not seen in this verse is the burden upon the parent to teach obedience. The parent is not the only teacher but I think I can say with some assurance that the parent is the main teacher, especially the father; not the school or the church or the government, but the parents. If the father wants to raise godly children he would do well to look at the relationship between the Son of God and His Father. Let's look at just a couple of things taken from Hebrews, chapter 5: "Who in the days of his flesh, when he had offered up prayers and supplications with strong crying and tears unto him that was able to save him from death, and was heard in that he feared, though he were a Son, yet learned he obedience by the things which he suffered; and being made perfect, he became the author of eternal salvation unto all them that obey him" (vs. 7–9). It would be impossible for us to even scratch the surface of the great truths contained in this section but I think we can draw an obvious conclusion.

Obedience Is Learned

If the Son of God learned obedience then we can conclude that obedience is something that is learned. If obedience is something that is learned, it is something that must be taught. This isn't rocket science but I fear it is oftentimes overlooked in its simplicity.

The parent is responsible to teach obedience as much as the child is responsible to learn it. How did the Father teach obedience to the Son? Through the things that He suffered. Remember, obedience is something that is taught but the lessons aren't always easy. The eternal Son of God, the One Who existed before time began, was sent to earth to become mortal and subject to time. The self-existent, self-sufficient, stooped to becoming dependent on food and water, breath and even rest. The Son, in obedience to the Father's will, laid aside His heavenly status, was fashioned as a man, humbled Himself and became obedient unto death, even the death of the cross. (see Phil.2:7–8). The omniscient Son learned obedience as He lived and died obediently.

God the Son is not only learning obedience through these difficult lessons but He is also learning the love of the Father as well. "For what son is he whom the father chasteneth not?" (Heb.12:7b). If a man really loves his son and wants to teach him how to be godly, he won't avoid the hard lessons of life. In the world you are going to have tribulations and trials that will demand you hold fast to the truth of your convictions and do what is right in the face of some easier path. God the Father allowed His Son to suffer the rejection of men and that is not easy for any parent. "He was in the world, and the world was made by him, and the world knew him not. He came unto his own, and his own received him not" (Jn.1:10–11).

In the Garden of Gethsemane the Son prayed to His Father with tears and agony that He would deliver Him from the sufferings of the cross. The Father was more than able to deliver Him yet He allowed Him to suffer. Sometimes the love of the Father sees beyond the immediate to a greater and more complete solution. "For whom the Lord loveth he chasteneth, and scourgeth every son who he receiveth" (Heb.12:6). Chastening is something a parent should never enjoy. Something is seriously wrong with the parent if they find joy in chastening their child. "Now no chastening for the present seemeth to be joyous, but grievous; nevertheless afterward it yieldeth the peaceable fruit of righteousness unto them who are exercised by it" (Heb. 12:11). Yes, obedience is learned, even by the Son of God. Its lessons aren't always easy but I am glad the Father taught it and I'm glad the Son learned it.

Oh, the Blessing of Obedience

Abel obeyed God and offered an acceptable sacrifice for his sin. Noah obeyed God by building an ark and the world got a second chance. Abraham obeyed God and left his native home for a land of promise, when he didn't even know where he was going. When God tested Abraham he was even willing to offer up his son Isaac whom he loved. The patriarchs and fathers of our faith have passed on the blessing of God through their obedience to God. The ultimate blessing of God came through the obedience of the Lord Jesus at the cross. "That the blessing of Abraham might come on the Gentiles through Jesus Christ, that we might receive the promise of the Spirit through faith" (Gal.3:14). My very hope of eternal life was dependent on the obedience of Christ to the will of the Father. I will forever be indebted and grateful to God the Father for His great love for me; a love that would send His Son to earth and allow Him to suffer the pains of this old life so that through His obedience I could become a child of God through faith in Him. "For God so loved the world that he gave his only begotten Son that whosoever believeth in him should not perish but have everlasting life" (Jn.3:16).

If you have never received the blessing of obedience to the call of God through the gospel, then I urge you right now to humbly confess Christ as your Savior and Lord and ask Him to put His Holy Spirit in you. Ask Him to turn your heart toward a life of obedience to His Word and His ways. Ask God to help you grow strong in the faith as you press on in your new found life in Christ. "And it shall come to pass, that whosoever shall call on the name of the Lord shall be saved" (Acts 2:21). "For there is no difference between the Jew and the Greek; for the same Lord over all is rich unto all that call upon him. For whosoever shall call upon the name of the Lord shall be saved" (Rom.10:12–13).

What New Doctrine Is This

"And they went into Capernaum; and straightway on the Sabbath day he entered into the synagogue, and taught. And they were astonished at his doctrine; for he taught them as one that had authority, and not as the scribes. And there was in their synagogue a man with an unclean spirit; and he cried out, saying, Let us alone! What have we to do with thee, thou Jesus of Nazareth? Art thou come to destroy us? I know thee, who thou art, the Holy One of God. And Jesus rebuked him, saying, Hold thy peace, and come out of him. And when the unclean spirit had torn him, and cried with a loud voice, he came out of him. And they were all amazed, insomuch that they questioned among themselves, saying, What thing is this? What new doctrine is this? For with authority he commandeth even the unclean spirits, and they do obey him" (Mk.1:21-27). The simple truth is the doctrine wasn't new, but the whole issue of authority was, at least new to them. The unclean spirits were very familiar with the authority, but for most of the people at Capernaum it was astonishingly new. If parents are ever to teach obedience to their children, there needs to be a good understanding of biblical authority. We need to know what it is, how we get it, and how it is to be used. If we can return to biblical authority, we too may be astonished at His doctrine.

AUTHORITY

The simple definition of authority is: legal power to command. If you are in a bank and robbers come in with weapons and ski masks and command you to get on the floor and lay face down, OBEY! They have a measure of momentary power but they do not have the legal power to command. The legal power to command is based on the character, dignity and creditability of the authority. Those under authority willingly submit out of trust because they respect it and believe it to be right. God has established authority for the individual, the home, the church and the nation.

HOW DO WE GET AUTHORITY

Many people marveled at the ministry of Jesus. But there are only two times recorded in scripture where Jesus ever marveled at men;

#1 He marveled at people's unbelief, Mark 6:6.

#2 He marveled at a soldier's understanding of authority, Luke 7:9.

This account in Luke's gospel is one of the best when it comes to understanding authority.

The soldier in Luke 7 was a centurion, meaning he was in command of 100 men. He had a servant whom he loved that was sick and near death. He had heard of the ministry of Jesus and how many sick people were being healed. Having heard about Jesus it was possible for him to have faith. "How then shall they call on him in whom they have not believed? And how shall they believe in him of whom they have not heard?" (Rom.10:14a).

This particular centurion had a place in his heart for the Jews and had even helped finance the building of their synagogue. Having heard that Jesus was a Jew and might be somewhat reluctant to come and help a Gentile he entreated some of the leading Jews to see if they might persuade Jesus to come to his home and heal his servant. Let's pick up the narrative at verse 6: "Then Jesus went with them. And when he was now not far from the house, the centurion sent friends to him, saying unto him, Lord, trouble not thyself; for I am not worthy that thou shouldest enter under my roof. Wherefore, neither thought I myself worthy to come unto thee; but say in a word, and my servant shall be healed. For I also am a man set under authority, having under me soldiers, and I say unto one, Go; and he goeth; and to another, Come; and he cometh; and to my servant, Do this; and he doeth it. When Jesus heard these things, he marveled at him, and turned him about, and said unto the people that followed him, I say unto you, I have not found so great faith, no, not in Israel" (Lk.7:6–9).

The centurion had authority over his men only because he himself was under the authority of a superior. The centurion knew that his authority was only as powerful as the authority he was under. Ultimately his authority came from Rome, the greatest power on earth at that time. He also knew that he was dealing with an issue that needed a greater power than Rome. His servant was about to die and only God could spare his life. He recognized that because Jesus was under the authority of Almighty God, He could exercise authority over life and death. He came to this understanding and faith just before Jesus was to arrive at his house. He didn't want Jesus to come under his roof for he knew symbolically that coming under his roof would be like coming under his authority. This soldier embraced a lot of truth in a short time and it paid off. Jesus marveled at his understanding and credited it to his faith.

The Authority of Christ

Jesus had authority and everyone knew it. He commanded the wind and the waves and they obeyed Him. He called Lazarus from the tomb and he obeyed Him. He healed all manner of sickness and disease, gave sight to the blind, hearing to the deaf, speech to the dumb, and mobility to the lame. He cast out demons, cleansed lepers and fed multitudes with five loaves and two fishes. We can't say enough about His authority, but we can't forget the secret to His authority. He was under the authority of His Father. "For I came down from heaven, not to do mine own will, but the will of him that sent me" (Jn.6:38). In the Garden of Gethsemane He beseeched the Father that all things were possible if He would just let the cup of suffering pass from Him, nevertheless "not My will but Thine be done." Jesus would have the authority over sin and death only as long as He remained under the authority of the Father. Jesus stood before Pilate who told Jesus that he had the authority to crucify Him or release Him. Jesus looked him in the eyes and told him he had no authority over Him at all unless the Father who sent Him gave him authority. No man had the authority to forcibly take the life of Jesus. He was going to lay it down under the authority of the Father. Having laid it down willingly, He would also take it up again. As Jesus was about to return to heaven having finished the work that the Father had sent Him to do, He said these words to His disciples, "And Jesus came and spake unto them, saying, All authority is given unto me in heaven and in earth. Go ye therefore, and teach (with authority) all nations, baptizing them in the name of the Father, and of the Son, and of the Holy Spirit; teaching them to observe all things whatsoever I have commanded you; and, lo, I am with you alway, even unto the end of the world, Amen" (Matt. 28:18–20).

Authority in the Home

In raising godly children it is imperative that both the parents and the children understand who the authority is in the home. Christ is the head of the Christian home. All authority in heaven and in earth is given unto Him. If the father wants to teach his children as one having authority and not as the scribes, he himself must be under the authority of Christ. If a man has no authority over his own soul, how can he teach with authority in his own home? If a man has no authority in his own home, how can he rule in the house of God which is the church? If there is no authority in the church, is it any wonder that we have so little salt and light to offer a wayward nation?

The order of this legal power to command is best seen in Paul's first letter to Timothy. Timothy was given the task of setting things in order in the churches of Asia. In Paul's list of qualifications for church leaders he sets out the order of authority. "This is a true saying; if a man desireth the office of a bishop, he desireth a good work. A bishop then must be blameless, the husband of one wife, temperate, sober-minded, of good behavior, given to hospitality, apt to teach; not given to wine, not violent, not greedy of filthy lucre, but patient, not a brawler, not covetous" (1 Tim.3:1–3). First of all these words describe a man who is under the authority of Christ in his own life. He can command his own soul which is the first requirement in the structure of authority. A man who has fought against God in his life and lost to the power of the gospel, has really won. "For whosoever will save his life shall lose it; but whosoever shall lose his life for my sake and the gospel's, the same shall save it" (Mk. 8:35).

When a man submits and places himself under the authority of God in his life he will have the power of God to first command his own soul. Having command of his own soul, he has the legal right to teach with authority in his own home. This is explained in the next two verses. "One that ruleth well his own house, having his children in subjection with all gravity, for if a man know not how to rule his own house, how shall he take care of the church of God?" (1 Tim.3:4,5). A husband under the authority of God in his own life will make it his first priority to have fellowship in the spirit with his wife. When sin occurs and fellowship is broken, they humble themselves and bring God into the center of the mix. They hold hands and pray for mercy and grace to help them regain fellowship. If the man is to fulfill his role as spiritual leader in the home ["For the husband is the head of the wife, even as Christ is the head of the church; and he is the savior of the body" (Eph.5:23)], he would be wise to lead out in humility and face sin head on. Sin would love to destroy his home and it will be if it is ignored.

The man has the position of authority in the home but if he is not under the authority of God in his own life he will only have the authority of the scribes. He will not have the astonishing kind of authority that Jesus had. He will have the legal right to command but he will lack the power that comes from being under the authority of God. The legal power to command that is based on character, dignity and credibility is the kind that wives and children submit to because it is respected and believed to be right. "Husbands, love your wives, even as Christ also loved the church, and gave himself for it, that he might sanctify and cleanse it with the washing of water by the word; That he might present it to himself a glorious church, not having spot, or wrinkle, or any such thing; but that it should be holy and without blemish. So ought men to love their wives as their own bodies. He that loveth his wife loveth himself" (Eph. 5:25–28).

A man's esteem for Christ is best seen in how he treats his wife, how he speaks of her to others and how he speaks to her in private. When children see their father cherish and honor their mother, it's not difficult for them to do the same. When children see their parents submitting themselves to one another in the fear of God, it gives credibility, dignity and character to their authority. The legal power comes from above and children submit because they respect it and believe it to be right.

Not as the Scribes

Jesus taught them as One having authority and not as the scribes. The scribes had developed a complicated mass of rules and regulations that basically governed all of Jewish life. The people were worn out trying to keep the rules and whenever they could they would ignore them. They taught certain ways to wash pots and cups and many other such things. The scribes talked the talk of worship but their hearts were far from God. Everyone knows that rules without a relationship will produce rebellion. It is true in our personal life, in marriage, the family, the church and the government. The scribes had rejected the Word of God in their own lives and substituted it with rules and traditions which made the Word of God useless to them or their children. This same sad process is repeated in many homes. Unless the head of the family places themselves under the authority of God in their own life they will never be able to command their own soul, let alone have any authority over those they are entrusted to teach. Again, they will be like the scribe who has the legal right to command, but will lack the power that comes from being under the authority of the gospel.

There are some who may be disappointed in the lack of *do's* and *don'ts* in this chapter, but I must confess it has been done deliberately. I believe if a man places himself under God's authority, God Himself will custom design the guidelines for his home regardless of the culture or century in which he is living.

CHAPTER FOUR

Blessing Your Family

About twenty years ago Joyce read a book about blessing one's family. She wanted me to look at it and see if I thought it might be something we should consider doing with our children. For whatever reason I didn't look at it and eventually forgot all about it. Three or four years later we heard some teaching on it again. We decided to look into it together to see if the Lord might have us bless our children. We found it to be something profitable in our family journey and include these thoughts for your consideration.

Research and Decision

Word Study; The Hebrew word for "bless" is *barak*. Its Greek equivalent is *eulogeo*. To bless means to endow with power for success, prosperity, fecundity, longevity, etc. Its major function seems to have been to confer an abundant and effective life upon someone or something. God is the only source of blessing and as such controls all blessing and cursing. It is His presence that confers blessing and it is only in His Name that others can confer blessing (see Deut. 10:8). Indeed, God's Name is the manifestation of His personal redemptive covenant keeping nature and is at the heart of all blessing. (A much more detailed definition of bless is found in Harris/Archer/Waltke 1988, "Theological Word Book of the Old Testament," page 132.)

Quite honestly the word *bless* wasn't much clearer to me after the study than it was before. I asked the Lord to guide me and set out to look at it in scripture. To my surprise the word *bless* is used over 500 times in Scripture. Many times David seems to direct the word toward God during a time of worship. "The Lord liveth; and blessed be my rock; and let the God of my salvation be exalted" (Ps.18:46). "Blessed be the Lord, because he hath heard the voice of my supplications" (Ps.28:6). "I will bless the Lord at all times; his praise shall continually be in my mouth" (Ps. 34:1). "Thus will I bless thee while I live; I will lift up my hands in thy name" (Ps.63:4). "Oh bless our God, ye people, and make the voice of his praise to be heard" (Ps.66:8). There are many such examples in the Psalms and something Christians would do well to practice.

There are numerous New Testament examples as well. "And the multitudes that went before, and that followed, cried, saying, Hosanna to the Son of David! Blessed is he that cometh in the name of the Lord! Hosanna in the highest!" (Matt.21:9). "Blessed be God, even the Father of our Lord Jesus Christ, the Father of mercies, and the God of all comfort" (2 Cor.1:3). "Blessed be the God and Father of our Lord Jesus Christ, who hath blessed us with all spiritual blessings in heavenly places in Christ" (Eph. 1:3). "And every creature that is in heaven and on the earth, and under the earth, and such as that are in the sea, and all that are in them, heard I saying, Blessing, and honor, and glory, and power, be unto him that sitteth upon the throne, and unto the Lamb for ever and ever" (Rev.5:13). As I began to examine the numerous references in scripture I asked myself the question if there might be something I had missed, some concept, some act of obedience in a spoken word of blessing.

What About the Curse?

The opposite of *to bless* is *to curse;* both seem to be significantly powerful. The power of execution seems to have been carried in the curse. When Adam sinned, the curse of death came upon him and all his descendants. A curse is a powerful thing; remember the fig tree, "And Peter calling to remembrance saith unto him, Master, behold the fig tree which thou cursed is withered away" (Mk. 11:21). It is interesting that Jesus just spoke a curse on the barren fig tree and immediately it withered.

God broke the curse of man's sin with a blessing. The blessing had been in the form of a promise made to Adam, carried down to Abraham and his descendants. The promise was eventually fulfilled in the person of the Lord Jesus Christ who was made a curse for us that He might redeem us from the curse of the law… that the blessing of Abraham might come to the Gentiles through Jesus Christ, (see Gal.3:13–14).

The Sermon on the Mount included these words: "But I say unto you, love your enemies, bless them that curse you, do good to them that hate you, and pray for them that despitefully use you, and persecute you" (Matt. 5:44). "Bless them who persecute you; Bless and curse not" (Rom.12:14). There seems to be at least a hint that a blessing is more powerful than a curse and possibly a blessing can even short circuit a curse allowing the intended blessing to be ours. "Not rendering evil for evil, or railing for railing, but on the contrary, blessing, knowing that ye are called to inherit a blessing" (1 Pet.3:9). I make no claim to understand all the spiritual dynamics of this but I felt led to press on toward blessing my family.

The Scripture that moved me the most and brought me to the place of commitment to one day bless our children is found in the gospel of Mark. Jesus is ministering in Judea near the Jordon. Due to the increasing popularity of Jesus' healing and teaching ministry, much of the disciples' ministry had turned to working crowd control for the people would press to get near Him, even just to touch Him. A group of mothers were trying to get their children to Jesus so He would touch them. Jesus noticed the disciples seem to indicate that the Lord had no time to be bothered with them. Let's pick up the narrative, "And they brought young children to him, that he should touch them; and his disciples rebuked those that brought them. But when Jesus saw it, he was much displeased, and said unto them, Permit the little children to come unto me, and forbid them not; for such is the kingdom of God. Verily I say unto you, Whosoever shall not receive the kingdom of God as a little child, he shall not enter into it. And he took them up in his arms, put his hands upon them, and blessed them" (Mk.10:13–16). In the Hebrew custom this was the act of a father. When Jacob deceived his father Isaac and stole Esau's spoken blessing, Esau was extremely distraught over it. "And Esau said unto his father, Hast thou but one blessing, my father? Bless me, even me also, O my father. And Esau lifted up his voice and wept" (Gen 27:38). I am sure there was much more understanding to the significance of a spoken blessing in the days of the patriarchs than we have in our modern days with our western glasses on. But with our study of the Scriptures both Joyce and I felt urged to press on and see how the Lord would lead us.

How Does a Person Receive a Blessing

Obedience is one way to receive a blessing. "Behold, I set before you this day a blessing and a curse; A blessing, if you obey the commandments of the Lord your God, which I command you this day; and a curse, if ye will not obey the commandments of the Lord your God, but turn aside out of the way which I command you this day, to go after other gods, which you have not known" (Deut.11:26–28). Another way to receive a blessing is to be a blessing. "Not rendering evil for evil, nor railing for railing, but on the contrary, blessing, knowing that ye are called to this, that ye should inherit a blessing" (1 Pet.3:9, see also Matt 5:44 and Rom 12:14). Another way of receiving a blessing is by having one bestowed upon us, such as a father blesses his children. Isaac blessed Jacob and Jacob blessed his grandsons, Ephraim and Manasseh. "By faith Jacob, when he was a dying, blessed both the sons of Joseph, and worshipped, leaning upon the top of his staff" (Heb.11:21).

How Does a Father Bless His Family

#1 Isaac kissed Jacob before he blessed him and he also put his hand on his head. A proper and meaningful touch is something that is important to everyone in the family especially at a time of special blessing.

#2 The power of life and death are in the tongue, and by a man's words he is justified or condemned. Therefore, carefully chosen words and prayed over words need to be spoken at the time of blessing. We felt led of the Lord to avoid any possible mention of some past shortcoming that might hinder our children in receiving the blessing we were intending to give.

#3 The blessing would focus on honor. We wanted the blessing to be a time of communicating the high value each child has to God and to us. We look upon our children as a great blessing from the Lord and this was to be a significant reminder, an acknowledgement of the high esteem in which we hold His design for the family.

#4 We asked the Lord to lead us to a particular character quality that would best suit a blessing for each child. We found this to be a great adventure in prayer. Moreover, we found it was given powerfully to each child as an individual. We included a promise to faithfully uphold them in prayer as they pressed on in their journey of life.

The Blessing Worksheet

✧ BIRTH – In this opening, express joy over the following details; the month, day and year they were born; the time of day or night; whether at home or the hospital or on the way to the hospital; how long their mother was in labor; details about their name, its meaning and/or who they may be named after; where they are in the birth order; what country, state, county, city in which they were born. Again, express joy!

✧ EARLY YEARS – Continue on expressing honor, appreciation, affirmation and acceptance. Pray for the right choice of words. Use language that promotes relational values. This is a good place to mention some special characteristics, i.e. whether they are quiet or loud, shy or adventurous, obedient or mischievous.

- ✧ SPIRITUAL GIFT – If your children are young you may not know their spiritual gift(s). Do some reading on how to discern spiritual gifts and pray for the Lord's help. If you are uncertain of their spiritual gift, then say so and move on. Don't choose one for them, let God do that. He is the One Who gives gifts. If you are quite certain then tell them what a great privilege it is to have that particular gift and give them any insights you can on how to stir it up and use it for God's glory.

- ✧ CHARACTER STRENGTHS – Remember, this is not the place to mention any weaknesses, the focus here is strength. Husband and wife should spend time discussing their child's strengths. Character is usually something that develops during difficulties and reveals itself in a crisis.

- ✧ GIVE A CAUTION – If possible, mention something they are already working on or have conquered. In an attitude of grace, focus more on the benefits of caution than the consequences of neglect. The apostle makes several references to cautions: "I write not these things to shame you, but as my beloved sons I warn you" (1 Cor.4:14).

- ✧ BESTOW A BLESSING – By this point our hearts are prepared to hear from the Lord the blessing He would have us bestow upon our child. Be willing to be still and wait on the Lord for His guidance and direction. On two occasions, by His grace, I was privileged to spend the entire night waiting on the Lord until I felt I had the direction I needed for their blessing.

Example of a Blessing

The special day of blessing came on March 20th, 1995. Joyce is a master of building anticipation and we all gathered at our home to enjoy a specially prepared meal. Joyce is also a great cook! Ben and Carmen brought baby Natalie, our only grandchild at that time. The rest of our children were unmarried and still home. I nervously told the children the time had come for us to do what we had been planning for some months. We all sat around in a circle in the downstairs family room. I explained that I would read some things that I had prepared for each of them and then at the time of pronouncing the blessing I would stand behind them and place my hand on their head and read their blessing. Ben is the first one so I will use him as an example.

Benjamin, son of my right hand, our firstborn. You came to your mother and me July 11th 1971, at 12:35am. You weighed 8 lbs.,14½ oz. and were 21 inches long. Your mother was in labor for 9 hours and you were born in St. Luke's Hospital in Marquette, Michigan. Your middle name, Dexter, comes from your great grandfather's older brother who died at the age of 19 from an epidemic that was sweeping the South. Dexter was always referred to as a fine young man and all his younger brothers and sisters loved him. Aunt Iva Lee said she cried for days when Dexter passed away. I'm glad Grandpa, you and I have this middle name in common.

Ben, I want to thank you for being such a good example to the rest of our children. Being the firstborn made it natural for you to be looked up to but it also made many situations in life inescapably on display. I congratulate you for not only enduring that aspect of your birth order but also for excelling in the great majority of your trials while growing up. As we watched you move into adulthood, we could see that many of the good decisions you made in your younger years were beginning to pay off. You have not only won the respect of your brothers and sisters, but also your parents. Thank you for being such a good example of the power of Christ so obviously working in a person's life.

As Mom and I have seen you grow spiritually, it has been a joy to see your spiritual gift of exhortation emerge. As an exhorter you are committed to spiritual growth in yourself as well as in others. You have an ability to see root problems as well as the necessary steps of solving them. As an exhorter you will gain most of your insights through personal study and experience. My encouragement to you is twofold: (1). Romans 12:12 "Rejoicing in hope, patient in tribulation, continuing diligently in prayer. (2). 2 Timothy 1:6 "Wherefore I put thee in remembrance that thou stir up the gift of God, which is in thee…" Provide yourself with good Christian friends, good preaching, good books and good spiritual disciplines like scripture memory and meditation. Develop your gift as long as God gives you life and know that He has a purpose for it.

Jesus grew in wisdom and in stature and in favor with God and man. Your mother and I have really enjoyed seeing you grow intellectually. You think! I have been amazed on more than one occasion seeing you logically work through things and figure out the best course of action. I admire the way God has taught you to look at things and think them through. Continue to think before you act and God will protect you from foolishness.

Your character strengths are: *Availability* as opposed to self-centeredness. *Creativity*—approaching a need or task or an idea from a new perspective. *Resourcefulness*—wise use of that which others would normally overlook or discard. *Thriftiness*—Not letting yourself or others spend that which is not necessary. *Sincerity*—eagerness to do what is right with transparent motives. Continue to add virtue to your faith and you will always prosper in all that you do (2 Peter 1:5–10).

Before I pronounce your blessing, let me give you one caution: Be alert to danger. Jesus asked His favored disciples to watch and pray so they wouldn't enter into temptation. Be careful to protect the things you value the most: your faith, your family and your future. How well we all know the enemy lurks about seeking to destroy any unsuspecting soul.

At this point I got up and stood behind him placing my right hand on his head as he sat in his chair. I prayed the following blessing. "Dear Heavenly Father, I pray that You would be pleased to confer with me the blessing of contentment upon Benjamin. Bless him with the heart of the apostle Paul who said in Philippians 4:11 "…I have learned, in whatever state I am in, to be content" May he have a strong awareness that You have provided everything he needs for his present happiness. Bless him with a fuller understanding about godliness with contentment being great gain. May his contented heart become a great blessing to his wife and children. And, Ben, as distinctly as a uniform identifies a soldier, may the unmistakable radiance of contentment be evident in your countenance, your conduct and your conversation."

The Effect

The next blessing was given to our daughter-in-law, Carmen. Here is a good and godly young wife and mother. Having married into a family uncertain of how she fits, her blessing was a time of affirmation, letting her know how much she is loved, accepted and appreciated. Our daughter, Ellen, was next and by this time there was a hallowed atmosphere of anticipation of what blessing the Father might have for her. By this time we all had tender hearts and moist eyes. Though each blessing was unique, we continued to follow the same basic format. Unknown to Joyce, I had prepared a special blessing for her. The children were thrilled as their mother was honored and blessed. It was as if all of us joined together in holding her in high esteem. "Her children rise up and call her blessed; her husband also, and he praiseth her" (Prov.31:28). As our time of blessing concluded, Ben asked if I had prepared a blessing for baby Natalie, I said I hadn't but I felt prompted to pray the Aaronic blessing that I had just memorized. Ben handed her to me and I held her up as we all stood close around. "The Lord bless thee and keep thee; The Lord make his face shine upon thee, and be gracious unto thee; The Lord lift up his countenance upon thee and give thee peace" (Num.6:24–26).

The Conclusion

I don't think it is within the scope of our imagination to comprehend the results of a blessing. Spiritual dynamics are always difficult to measure, but I think this simple act of obedience to the leading of the Lord has contributed to the overall shape and success of our family relationships these many years later. As time went on and the rest of our children married, they with one consent asked if we could have a special time of blessing for their mate, which we were honored to do. We now have a special time of blessing for our grandchildren at our family consecration which is explained in our next chapter. As I look back over my shoulder I sense it was a simple act of obedience to God's leading. I think He was glorified and we were edified.

CHAPTER FIVE

A Family Consecration

Joyce and I were headed out East for a speaking engagement and had been in the car for quite a spell. Often times we read to each other or listen to tapes. This time though we had been quietly thinking for some time. I broke the silence with a question. I asked her if she could do anything she wanted, what would it be? She answered quickly though thoughtfully. She said she would like to do something special with our children once a year that would be spiritually focused; something that would strengthen our faith in Christ as a family. My heart resonated with her words so we began to pray and seek the Lord's leading.

Our itinerant ministry has us in the car a lot and we try to make good use of the time as much as possible. Our next few trips became planning sessions. We knew one of the first things we would need is a name for the event. We chose the name, "A Family Consecration." The word *consecration* means to be set apart unto the Lord. We weren't quite sure what we would do but we knew we wanted it to include a time of consecrating ourselves to the Lord and the things of His Word. As we shared our thoughts with the children they got excited and said they would pray with us as we planned.

First Time for Everything

Some friends of ours told us they had just been to Gatlinburg for a few days with their children and really enjoyed it. We decided Gatlinburg would be a good place to begin. We found a rental house that would accommodate us for three days at a reasonable price. We felt if we were going to suggest the venture we should be responsible for the cost of the accommodations. We set a date right after Labor Day and began to make preparations. We planned to have evening devotions as well as a little Scripture memory challenge. A small prize would be given to all who could quote some scripture. Our family likes to sing so we took some song books and Ben brought his guitar. We planned to have a family communion service led by Dad. As the evening drew to a conclusion we would all sing, "Take My Life and Let It Be Consecrated Lord to Thee." The song has become a yearly tradition and a good one. Though the song is much easier to sing than it is to live, it is our earnest desire to have a family that is consecrated to the ways of the Lord.

We enjoyed great meals, played table games and walked the streets of Gatlinburg. We took a picnic and went to Cades Cove. The weather was beautiful. The autumn colors were beginning to turn and we enjoyed creation and our Creator. We took lots of photographs and planned to make a photo album for each year. This has been a special blessing as we have seen our family grow in number and depth of relationship with each other and the Lord. All in all we felt our first family consecration was a success and were agreed we would like to do something similar each year.

As Time Went On

As time went on more structure just seemed to develop. As the remainder of our children married and had families of their own, it became more of a challenge to juggle schedules and make this thing work. Dates and reservations had to be made further in advance. Joyce organized the meals and all the girls helped. Each evening a different family would prepare a special evening meal. Breakfast was usually a leisurely continental meal of fruit, cereal and rolls. Joyce usually was responsible for lunch which often included leftovers from the day before. Joyce saw to it that our family consecrations were a time of feasting and not fasting.

Each lunch a different family planned a guessing game with some silly prize for winning: a box of cup cakes for guessing how many acorns were in the quart jar or how many pine needles were tied in a bundle. After the evening meal grandpa or an aunt or uncle would tell a Bible story. This also gave time for the remaining adults to cleanup and prepare for the evening activities. We made sure amidst the games, swimming, treasure hunts and scheduled activities, there was also free time for families to see something of interest on their own. The evening times were filled with rhythm band time for the smaller children, Scripture memory, hymns and songs. We shared testimonies and prayer requests. When the younger children were put to bed, one of the men would share something he had prepared from the Word. Each year it became more and more a time of spiritual refreshment. It became something each of us looked forward to.

Our first few years we had three day consecrations, but it eventually turned into five days and then on our seventh year we spent seven days in a family reunion lodge at the East gate of Yellowstone National Park. Each year we chose a theme. The Yellowstone theme was "Riding High in Our Western Adventure." We all wore cowboy hats and Joyce made the small boys chaps and vests. She also made little outfits for our cowgirls. We had a picnic in the city park in Cody, Wyoming, followed by a great rodeo later that evening. We had good fun and made great memories. Even now when we look at our photo albums we're reminded of these special times. There is plenty of work involved, but it is so small in comparison to the vastness of the treasures we take away.

Activities

Each year a different family would be responsible for the games. Depending on the time of year different games were chosen. Though most of our consecrations have been during warm weather, one year we went in the winter. We sledded, skated and snowballed every day. For most of our summertime ventures we have had access to a lake. Fishing, boating, and swimming are always favorites. We have played football, softball, soccer, big ball and all kinds of relay races and scavenger hunts. We also have many different table games that we enjoy.

We have found that family quizzes are both fun and beneficial. We made up a list of all our names and birthdays and had to draw a line matching the correct name to the correct birthday. We made a list of names leaving out the middle name and had to fill in the blanks. We even included grandparents and great-grandparents. We've had a quiz on wedding anniversaries. We've had a quiz on remembering the theme of each consecration and matching it with the year and location. Some of the places we have visited are: Williamsburg, Virginia; Gatlinburg, Tennessee; Pahaska Tepee, Wyoming; Mackinac Island, Eagle Harbor, Trout Lake, Indian Lake and Copper Harbor all in Michigan's Upper Peninsula. We have enjoyed all of them and found our greatest joy in just being together.

We have enjoyed telling stories of our in-laws and outlaws complete with a photo album full of old pictures of our ancestors which stretches back several generations. We have found that telling stories of our great-grandparents and grandparents gives all of us a sense of belonging. Stories of the past also give us a consciousness of the brevity of life, which we have found lends greater value to the present. It may seem a small thing but one we believe helps us find our place in this brief vapor that is called life. We try to bear in mind that we are not having activities for activities' sake—there is enough of that. Our desire is to enhance our family's relationship with God and each other.

Two Secrets to Success

The first secret to success is prayer. There is not a day of my life I do not pray about our family consecration. It has become that important to us. I pray for God's blessing and guidance. I pray for health and protection. I pray against the enemy's schemes to oppose it. I pray about the theme and location. I pray for the children's schedules and even the weather. Both Joyce and I take seriously the admonition of scripture; "Be anxious for nothing, **but in everything**, by prayer and supplication with thanksgiving let your requests be made known unto God" (Phi.4:6, emphasis mine). We have a consecration once a year and for eleven months I pray for the details concerning it. Then for the entire month after the consecration, I ask for nothing but only give thanks for His faithfulness in hearing and answering prayer. The Lord is so good, bless and praise His Holy Name!

The second secret is planning and organization. We get with the children far enough in advance to see what date will work best. We put it on the calendar and send them a letter as soon as we decide on a theme and make reservations. There have been two times in the past where some of the family couldn't come. Once, Ben and his family were on a year and a half mission trip in Africa. Another time, Gabriel was on military duty for a year in Iraq. Understanding things like this will happen and accepting it is key. Flexibility is a must in planning and organization. We needed a schedule for general guidance; one that served us, not one that we served.

Our schedule would include information on arrival times, meal times and menus, free times, who's responsible for little children's story time, and the adult who assists with crowd control. We always have one night for adults only. After all the little children have gone to bed, Joyce speaks from her heart to all the girls and I speak to all the guys. This is a special time of sharing and prayer.

We include information on who is to lead communion that year so they will have adequate time to prepare. Each year a different head of the household brings a special message from God's Word, something they have recently learned and feel would be beneficial. We have recommended portions of Scripture each year but give each one liberty to memorize whatever they desire. There are small cash prizes for the adults who memorize anything over 25 verses as well as for the children who memorize verses. Quoting Scripture has become a blessing to all of us and the reward of it is more precious than gold, yea than much fine gold. Prayer is really key as you organize and plan. The Lord seems to speak clearer to Joyce on the planning especially since her spiritual gift is organization.

As Children Grow Older

As our first-born grandchild began nearing the age of twelve we wanted to do something special for her. She was becoming a fine young lady and we wanted to have an event that would be remembered in her life as a time when she was looked upon not so much as a child, but as a young woman; something spiritual that would encourage her in her walk with the Lord.

Jesus was at the age of twelve when He was found by His parents in the temple debating with the PhDs of His day. He would listen to them and to their amazement He would ask them questions that indicated He had understanding beyond His years. Maybe as He entered Jerusalem His parents reminisced about the first time they came with Him to Jerusalem when He was only eight days old. It was then godly old Simeon took Him up in his arms and blessed Him saying that his eyes had seen the Lord's salvation. One thing for certain is this trip to Jerusalem at the age of twelve brought about an obvious awakening to spiritual things. Henceforth Jesus would be consecrated to His Father's business.

We told Natalie that we wanted to have a special service for her at the following consecration. We would call it a "Celebration of Lights" ceremony. I designed some helpful certainties about God and life from the Bible. I asked her if she would be willing to study and memorize them. She would be given a list of questions and answers to study from. She would study them with her parents and on a special evening at consecration she would be asked to share some of the things she had learned. She agreed and plans began to be made. Once again, we didn't have a pattern so we didn't know if we were doing it right. The following is copy of the study sheet she was given.

Helpful Certainties About God and Life From the Bible

Certainties About God

1.	He is eternal	Isa 57:15	He inhabiteth eternity.
2.	He is holy	Isa 6:3	The angels call Him holy.
3.	He is a spirit	John 4:24	God is a spirit and must be worshipped in spirit and truth.
4.	He is just	Deut 32:4	His ways are perfect.
5.	He created all things	Col 1:16–17	For by Him were all things created
6.	He is merciful	Ps 89:1	His mercy endureth forever
7.	He is loving and kind	1 Jn 4:7	Love is of God

Certainties About Man

1.	Man was made by God	Gen 2:7 Ps 100:3	It is He who hath made us
2.	Man entered into sin	Gen 3:6	He ate the fruit of the forbidden tree
3.	Death passed upon all men	Rom 5:12	Death came because of Adam's sin
4.	Man can know God	2 Tim 1:12	I know whom I have believed

5.	Man can believe and be saved	Eph 2:8–9	By grace are ye saved through faith
6.	Man can have everlasting life	John 5:24	Believe on the Lord Jesus Christ

Certainties About Satan

1.	He was created by God	Gen 3:1	Which the Lord God had made
2.	He rebelled against God	Isa 14:12–15	He was cast out of Heaven
3.	He tempted man to sin	Gen 3:1–6	He got man to doubt God's Word
4.	He is a liar and a murderer	John 8:44	He told Eve she wouldn't die
5.	His doom is eternal	Rev 20:10	The Lake of Fire

Certainties About Jesus

1.	He is eternal God	Phil 2:6 Rev 1:8	The Alpha and Omega
2.	He was born of a virgin	Lu 1:26–38	His mother's name was Mary
3.	He alone paid the price of our sin	Heb 1:2–3 2 Cor 5:21	By Himself purged our sins
4.	He is the Savior	Lu 2:11	He came to save the lost
5.	He is full of grace	John 1:14,16	He gives us grace
6.	He is King of Kings	Rev 17:14	He rules the heaven and earth
7.	He is coming to earth again	John 14:1–3 Acts 1:11	In the clouds with great glory

Certainties About the Holy Spirit

1. He lives in the bodies of Christians	1 Cor 6:19	Not man-made temples
2. He is our teacher and guide	Jn 14:16–18	He guides us into truth
3. He is our comforter	John 14:26, 16:13	He will not leave us comfortless
4. He speaks to our spirit	Rom 8:14–17	His inner voice to our inner man
5. He is God's proof of salvation	Rom 8:9 Eph 4:30	His promise and seal

Know the Simple Gospel

Memorize	1 Corinthians 15:3–4 Romans 10:9–10
Man's Eternal State	The Redeemed – Col 1:5 The Lost – Matt 25:41
Our Purpose in Life	To glorify God and enjoy Him forever – 1 Cor 10:31, Phil 4:4
Can I know if I am saved?	Yes –1 John 5:13–15, John 10:27–29, 2 Tim 1:12

Ceremony of Lights Celebration

We had a special meal for her "Celebration of Lights" ceremony. Each one of the adults had been given a question to ask her with regards to the things she had studied. She said she was nervous but acted as cool as a cucumber. Beginning with her parents and followed by grandparents, aunts and uncles, each asked their question or questions as they saw fit. After this portion was complete, each couple got up one at a time and gave her a blessing and a special gift in memory of the occasion. Joyce had read through a woman's study Bible and filled it with personal notes to Natalie. Both Joyce and I are reading through Bibles personalizing them with grandchildren in mind. We will be presenting these to them at their ceremony. Joyce is doing one for the next granddaughter's ceremony and I for the next grandson's. It is such an incentive for us to keep reading our Bibles. It endears our grandchildren to us in ways we hadn't imagined. We can't think of a better gift to give them.

Some of the older grandchildren sat in on Natalie's ceremony. They were encouraged to begin looking forward to their time of celebration. Caleb and Levi were going to be of age in two years. We planned to call their ceremony, "Armor of Lights Celebration." We wanted the names of their ceremonies to be different because we believe there is a difference between boys and girls, men and women. We want to do all we can to encourage our young men to be men (masculine) and our young women to be women (feminine). We want them to be grateful to God for their gender and seek to glorify Him in the role He has given them.

Armor of Lights Celebration

By the time Caleb and Levi's celebration came around they were ready and raring to go. They knew what to expect. They had done the study and answered the questions. Natalie got to be in on the questions this time and she felt like a veteran. It was a great time of blessings and gifts for everyone involved. At times all of us were moved to tears at the depth of thoughts and concern shown for the boys. It became a time when they knew more was going to be expected from them. Though they were still young they knew they were putting away some of the childish things and starting to put on the things of a man. "When I was a child, I spoke as a child, I understood as a child, I thought as a child, but when I became a man, I put away childish things" (1 Cor. 13:11). Growing into adulthood is a process marked with helps and hindrances. We as a family are beginning to see the value of this time as a special source of encouragement to keep pressing on to maturity. In a few months we will be celebrating our fourteenth family consecration and we have three grandchildren who will be having their ceremonies, one young lady and two young men. They are excited about it and so are we.

CHAPTER SIX

The Importance of Grand Parenting

One of the best portions of scripture on parenting and grand parenting is found in Hebrews 11:4–30. It is packed with powerful insights on faith, hope and love. It is filled with examples of how these truths are passed down through generations. "Lord, thou hast been our dwelling place in all generations" (Psa.90:1). If you have generations (plural), you have grandparents. One cannot be a grandparent without being a parent, neither can one be a parent without children, whether biological or adopted. The role of a grandparent is of necessity dependent upon children's children. "Children's children are the crown of old men; and the glory of children are their fathers" (Prov.17:6). Scripture has something to say about the joy and importance of grand parenting.

Jacob Loved His Grandchildren

My favorite grandparent verse is: "By faith Jacob, when he was a dying, blessed both the sons of Joseph, and worshipped, leaning upon the top of his staff" (Heb. 11:21). The Scriptural account of this in Genesis is too precious to omit: "And Israel beheld Joseph's sons, and said, Who are these? And Joseph said unto his father, They are my sons, whom God hath given me in this place. And he said, Bring them, I pray thee, unto me, and I will bless them. Now the eyes of Israel were dim for age, so that he could not see. And he brought them near unto him; and he kissed them, and embraced them. And Israel said unto Joseph, I had not thought to see thy face; and, lo, God hath shown me also thy seed. And Joseph brought them out from between his knees and bowed himself with his face to the earth. And Joseph took them both, Ephraim in his right hand toward Israel's left hand, and Manasseh in his left hand toward Israel's right hand, and brought them near unto him. And Israel stretched out his right hand, and laid it upon Ephraim's head, who was the younger, and his left hand upon Manasseh's head, guiding his hands knowingly; for Manasseh was the first born. And he blessed Joseph, and said, God, before whom my fathers Abraham and Isaac did walk, the God who fed me all my life long unto this day. The Angel who redeemed me from all evil, bless the lads; and let my name be named on them, and the name of my fathers Abraham and Isaac; and let them grow into a multitude in the midst of the earth" (Gen 48:8–16). The entire account can be read in Genesis 48:1–22.

"And when Jacob had made an end of commanding his sons, he gathered up his feet into the bed, and died, and was gathered unto his people" (Gen.49:33). He was one of the biblical old men who continued to be a blessing to his family right to the end of his journey which is something that should be important to all of us.

Poetry or Something More

Literary critics call Jacob's blessing; "Hebrew poetry of epic proportions." It would seem also appropriate to call it "grand parenting of epic proportions." Jacob, the patriarch, is about to finish well. He is near the end of his life and knows he has a sickness unto death. He wants to see his grandchildren for the last time and give them a spoken blessing. He hugs and kisses them in the presence of Joseph their father. It must have warmed Joseph's heart to see his father show affection for his children, especially when it was difficult for Jacob even to stand. Remember he was leaning on the top of his staff. Regardless of the difficulty, we have found there are few things that affirm your children as parents more than showing affection for their children. All of us need to have our roles affirmed. Affirming roles is a good ministry.

The part of Hebrews 11:21 that speaks the loudest to me is, "he worshiped." If Jacob is truly worshiping he must be doing it in spirit and in truth. This is no small thing for the man who had once wrestled with the angel of the Lord and said. "I will not let you go till you bless me." Jacob came away from that encounter with his name changed to Israel. Oh, to be a grandparent who wrestled with God so that at the end of his journey he can still worship and bless his grandchildren. It would seem from scripture that the root of his blessing had ramifications long after he was gone.

Ephraim and Manasseh grew up with all the advantages of Egyptian nobility. Their mother was the daughter of Potiphera, the priest of On. The priest of On was an important position surely accompanied by wealth and power (see Gen. 41:45). Yet

400 years later when Moses led the children of Israel out of Egypt the tribes of Ephraim and Manasseh were among them. Somewhere in the course of time they chose to leave the present luxuries of Egypt and by faith looked to their future life as Israelites. Scripture doesn't tell us when the decision was made to leave the comforts of aristocracy for the slavery of Goshen, but Scripture makes it clear that they did. I wonder what part Grandpa Jacob's blessing played in that decision and how often the story had been told to the next generations.

Future Generations

After Moses led the children of Israel across the Red Sea, they sent twelve spies to search out the Promised Land. For the most part we remember only the names of two of the spies. Caleb was from the tribe of Judah and Joshua was from the tribe of Ephraim, (see Num. 13). Joshua's character had been forged during the hard days of slavery, maybe even going back to the days when his forefathers had left freedom for bondage; a decision no one else could understand. Joshua was a mighty man of faith who eventually led the children of Israel in the conquest of Canaan. I wonder if Jacob could have imagined that generations later such a leader as Joshua would have come from his grandson Ephraim.

A Call From the Hospital

I just answered a call from Joyce. She is at the hospital. Brian and Kimberlee just delivered their seventh child, Ezra Brian Harmon, born at 4:45pm, 7lbs 14oz, 20 1/4 inches long, red curly hair and big hands. As Joyce was telling me the good news through her own deep emotions, in the background I could hear the cry of a newborn baby. Few things are as sacred as hearing the sound of an infant's first cry. Our hearts rejoiced at the birth of our 21st grandchild. Mother and baby are doing fine. I am off to the hospital to do something I have done with all our grandchildren. I'll write more later.

A Grandparent's First Prayer

I'm back from the hospital and ready to write on something that has become a tradition with all our grandchildren. It began with Natalie, our first grandchild. When Ben and Carmen first brought her over to the house and everyone had made a fuss over her, they handed her to me. I remember the feeling that I was holding another generation. I was so moved that I began to silently pray as if no one was in the room but the two of us. Joyce looked at me and said "You are praying, aren't you?" I told her, "Yes, and I am going to have this special silent prayer with all our grandchildren the first time I hold them." The tradition has almost become a sacred event with the parents handing me the child and saying, "Here, Dad" I look forward to it every time. Below is a copy of the prayer. I printed it out and then sign and date it so they can put it in their baby book.

#1 O Lord, I give you thanks for this child. "Lo, children are an heritage from the Lord; and the fruit of the womb is his reward" (Ps.127:3) Thankfulness always becomes us when we enter into prayer.

#2 O Lord, this child is a gift of Your grace, and we recognize that we are but stewards. We commit ourselves and this child to You. Dear Lord, we consecrate this child to You and Your service. (1 Peter 4:10 and Psalms 37:5).

#3 O Lord, please do not allow any of my sins or the sins of my children or my parents to be visited upon this child. In the powerful Name of the Lord Jesus and through His shed blood I break any generational curse where Satan might want to gain a foothold. Turn every evil desire Satan has back upon his wicked head a thousand fold. (see Exodus 20:5 and, Mark 9:14–29).

#4 Lord I pray Your blessing upon this child:
Bless them with salvation early in life – Romans 4:6–8
Bless them with a hunger and love for Your Word
– 1 Peter 2:2
Bless them with wisdom from above – James 1:5, 3:17
Bless them physically, mentally, emotionally, spiritually
and in every way that would glorify You
– Luke 2:40, 52
I pray the Aaronic blessing upon this child
– Numbers 6:24–26
Lord, please keep them from evil and the evil one
– John 17:15
Lord bless them with a humble and tender spirit
– Psalms 51:17

Being a Grandparent

Years ago we heard it said that you never really know if you have been a good parent until you see your grandchildren. We weren't really sure all that was intended in that statement, but we left thinking that we wanted our children to pass on the gospel of Christ to their children. If they raised good children, moral, honest, hard-working, reliable, etc., yet they never came to personal faith in Christ what would it profit? We believe if a person is godly he will be good, yet we also believe it is possible to be good without being godly. We came up with a phrase to remind each other of this: Being a parent or grandparent is easy, being a good parent or grandparent requires some effort and thought, being a godly parent or grandparent is impossible without God. "And Jesus looking upon them saith, With men it is impossible, but not with God; for with God all thing are possible" (Mk.10:27).

Joyce and I feel one of the greatest responsibilities we have as a grandparent is to pray for our grandchildren. We have a standard list of things we pray daily, as well as praying for individual needs as we become aware of them. When we have the privilege to watch them overnight we pray with them before they go to bed. We pray about spontaneous needs that may arise. We pray with them at meals times and in the car before they leave the driveway. There is a spiritual dynamic no one can measure when both parents and grandparents have a high priority on prayer. The earlier a child learns the importance of prayer, the greater their walk of faith will be. The more they learn to pray, the more they will escape the tempter's snare and stay on the path that pleases the Lord. "There hath no temptation taken you but such as is common to man; but God is faithful, who will not permit you to be tempted above what ye are able, but will with the temptation, also make a way of escape, that ye may be able to bear it" (1 Cor. 10:13). Prayer quenches a lot of the enemy's arrows before they ever leave the bow.

What Makes a Grandparent Grand?

When our children were growing up, Joyce became the master of gathering things that would lend them an advantage in their journey of faith. She made sure there were a number of good

Bible story books for them to read. She purchased all the story hour tapes by Aunt Sue and Uncle Dan. Each night she would put on a tape out in the hallway and the kids would fall asleep listening to a Bible story. We would listen to Ranger Bill, Patch the Pirate, and the Pacific Garden Mission's, "Unshackled." Today there are many good Bible story videos, books, board games and Christian radio programs available. They make great gifts and serve in developing a heart for the things of the Lord.

Learn to be a good listener. Give them your ear and genuinely take interest in what they are saying. Even when your grandchildren are small they can tell if you are really listening. Expect them to talk about things that interest them at their age. As a parent I missed opportunities in this area. I don't want to repeat that mistake with my grandchildren. We have learned if you give them your ears and your heart while they are young, they seem to return the favor when they get older. Winning a hearing is not easy at any age but it is important at every age.

Take advantage of the opportunities to be with them. When they come for a visit do what needs to be done to make your house grandchild friendly. Don't allow household things to become more important than making them feel loved and accepted. Michael, our son-in-law, made a cool toy box the kids filled with some of their old toys. The children forgot they were their old toys. They play with them at Grandma's like they were new.

We turned our back porch into a cowboy room with bunk beds and cowboy paraphernalia on the walls. When the boys were redoing the room for us we had them leave a small opening in the attic section and we call it "The Loft." It's about 8 feet off the ground about 4x4x3. You must be at least four years old to play in "The Loft," and the little ones eagerly await that special day. Parents sitting in the dining room can supervise from a cowboy mirror located on the far wall. All of the grandchildren have spent hours playing with small toys in "The Loft."

Trips with grandma and grandpa are big events. Being an itinerant preacher in churches, camps and conferences throughout the country gives us great opportunities to take our grandchildren with us. We started taking them at a young age. There were three qualifications for them to be able to go: they had to be potty trained, obey and sleep through the night. It is great when you have them one at a time but it is also fun for them to have a cousin along. Oh the memories we have made with them and how close they always feel to us after we have spent a week or so together. We take lots of pictures and tell lots of stories. We hike, swim, fish, visit points of interest, museums, battlefields, read historical markers, picnic, buy mementos and play table games with them.

We have found all of this kind of grand parenting takes a lot of prayer: prayer before, during and after; prayer for wisdom, grace, and protection. You never want a grandchild to be hurt on your watch. Remember grandparenting is easy, good grand parenting requires some effort and thought, but godly grand parenting is impossible without God.

Those Special Moments

This past summer Joyce was helping our daughter Ellen who was expecting. Meanwhile, I was speaking about four hours away. I took two of our grandsons, Caleb and Levi (age 13) along. We had a great time. I was praying for an opportunity to really make our time together special.

On the last day while eating at a country café, the thought occurred to me to ask them what they dreamed about. They looked at me kind of puzzled so I told them some of the dreams I had when I was going on fifteen. I dreamed of being a dairy farmer. I dreamed of being married and owning a farm house with a big red barn and large trees in the front yard. I dreamed of having a wife and children to share my life with. We would work together and eat our meals together.

As the boys shared some of their dreams I told them it was good to dream about the things in life. I told them hopes and dreams were helpful in a balanced life. I encouraged them to pray about their future dreams and ask the Holy Spirit to guide them in the right way they should go.

A couple of months later the boys earned some money. I asked them what they were going to do with it. One of the boys replied quickly by saying he was saving for a house. He had been dreaming. My mind went back to our special moment a few months earlier. Both Joyce and I pray for special moments with our grandchildren.

Seeing Him Who Is Invisible

Speak to your grandchildren about the heroes of faith who sought Him Who is invisible. "By faith Moses, when he was come to years, refused to be called the son of Pharaoh's daughter; choosing rather to suffer affliction with the people of God, than to enjoy the pleasures of sin for a season, esteeming the reproach of Christ greater riches than the treasures in Egypt; for he had respect unto the recompense of the reward. By faith he forsook Egypt, nor fearing the wrath of the king; for he endured, **as seeing him who is invisible**." (Heb. 11:24–27) (emphasis mine).

A good friend of mine related the following story to me. When his grandmother died his grandfather moved in with them. He slept in the same room with him and his two brothers. He was a Christian who read his Bible and prayed. He went to church and was active in church ministry. He lived with them for three years and then passed away. In all those years he never remembers his grandfather sharing the gospel or anything from the Bible with him.

Oh dear grandparents, never neglect the privilege and responsibility of sharing the glorious gospel with your grandchildren. Don't take the attitude that someone else will speak to them of Christ. Regardless if they have made a profession of faith, speak with them of the love of Christ and the power of the gospel. As they grow older share insights on gospel living that you have gained during your journey of faith. Be a loving reminder of the goodness of God in the life of Jesus Christ.

The high water mark of grand parenting is letting them know through word and deed that you genuinely care for their eternal souls. "Let the word of Christ dwell in you richly in all wisdom; teaching and admonishing one another in psalms and hymns and spiritual songs, singing with grace in your hearts to the Lord. And whatever ye do in word or deed, do all in the name of the Lord Jesus, giving thanks to God and the Father by him" (Col. 3:16–17).

CHAPTER SEVEN

Choices

Joyce and I have been inspired by men and women in Scripture who have made good choices. Their examples have been a great teaching tool for us in our own journey. We have also learned some things to avoid from the examples of those who have made bad choices. It would seem that God gives us the liberty to make whatever choices we want to make, but He doesn't give us the liberty to choose the consequences. We live with the consequences. Therefore with God's help, we determined to make choices that would most glorify Him.

Once we committed our lives to the Lord, we wondered how we could best serve Him. Some of the early Bible teaching we received encouraged us to make our marriage and family a top priority. We felt if our faith was real at home it would give us confidence for ministry to others. A godly family is also some of the best credentials for ministry outside the home. We soon became aware of the dangers in choosing a ministry focus. Any ministry can become an idol if it takes precedent over Christ. "Beware lest any man spoil you through philosophy and vain deceit, after the tradition of men, after the rudiments of the world, and not after Christ" (Col.2:8).

As we evaluated service for Christ we came to the conclusion that all other forms and avenues of ministry change throughout life, but one's covenant before God in marriage and family does not. We believe the transforming power of the gospel should first be evidenced not in the pulpit or the foreign mission field, but in the home. We know good people, sound in the faith, who disagree with this philosophy of ministry but we must all give account of ourselves before God. We continue to pray that our love and service for the Lord would be obvious in how we love and serve each other in our family. When our marriage and home pleases God—simply said—He gets the glory and we get the good.

Joshua

Joshua had been mentored by Moses and had also been appointed by God as Moses' successor to lead the children of Israel into the promise land. He had proven himself on the field of battle as a warrior, leader and commander. He was a man of prayer and sincerely tried to follow God in all his ways. He had seen the wonders that God performed in delivering the Israelites from Egypt. He had seen God's hand in providing and protecting them through their forty years of travel in the wilderness. He had seen the walls of Jericho fall. He was well recognized by Israel as God's man and leader of their nation.

When Joshua was an old seasoned veteran saint of God, he called for a special assembly of all the leaders of Israel. They were to meet in Shechem, the first place in Canaan to be mentioned in connection with Abraham's arrival. It was in Shechem that the Lord appeared to Abraham and promised the land to his descendants (see Gen 12:6–7). The stage was set perfectly for profound things to be said, things of great importance, things that would be remembered as guidelines for generations to come.

A Choice of Great Significance

"And if it seem evil unto you to serve the Lord, choose you this day whom you will serve; whether the gods which your fathers served that were on the other side of the river, or the gods of the Amorites, in whose land you now dwell; but as **for me and my house**, we will serve the Lord" (Josh. 24:15, emphasis mine). Joshua had just reviewed Israel's history, their past experience in the land of Egypt and the years of wilderness wanderings. A generation had just passed and another one was beginning. He wanted them to know that their future wasn't going to be left to chance but to choice. He told them he was going to write their decision in the book of the law of God and take a great stone and set it up under the oak that was by the sanctuary of the Lord as a witness to their choice. "And Joshua said unto all the people, Behold, this stone shall be a witness unto us; for it hath heard all the words of the Lord which he spoke unto us; it shall be therefore a witness unto you, lest you deny your God. So Joshua let the people depart, every man unto his inheritance" (Josh. 24:27–28). There was much at stake here and he wanted them to know it. Their homes, their lives and the very state of their nation would be affected by their choice. When the family drifts away from God's design, it begins to unravel and eventually the church and also the nation follow suit.

For Me and My House

There seems to be a lie that Satan has peddled throughout time. "The only person affected by a choice is the person who made the choice." The truth is, a choice always affects more than just the individual making it. It most often affects the people closest to us, the very people we love the most. If the choice is good, those we love benefit; but if it is bad, they suffer the consequences. Most parents realize this and make an effort to make choices that influence their children for good. Many parents make a choice to influence their children all they can in areas of sports, music, art, health, education, vocation, religion, etc. I am sure that Joshua and his wife were in agreement that they wanted their family to know and serve the Lord. Joshua knew this decision was right and, along with his family, could publicly declare his choice to the nation. His choice would be an encouragement to all who heard him and hopefully help establish Israel as a nation that loved and honored God in their homes.

Choose You This Day

Though Israel has not always been characterized by good choices, Israel was, and still is, God's choice. The covenant God established with Abraham and his descendants was that through him and Sarah all the nations of the world would be blessed. In fulfillment of Scripture, Jesus was the only one to choose His parents and He chose them from the nation of Israel of the house of David. Like most of us, David and his descendants had done their share of making good and bad choices, but David's best choice was obvious, he wanted to know and serve the Lord. In the fullness of time God made good His promise and sent the Lord Jesus into the world. He was both the Son of God and the son of man. He lived a perfect sinless life and yet one day died on the cross to pay the penalty for man's sin. The resurrection of Christ conquered the power of sin and death enabling all who believe to receive the gift of eternal life.

Sometimes we might think, "I'm not worthy to have eternal life." And God's reply to us is, "My child, I know; but My Son is eternally worthy to be called your Savior."

"Wherefore, as the Holy Spirit saith, Today if you will hear his voice, harden not your hearts, as in the provocation, in the day of trial in the wilderness when your fathers put me to the test, proved me and saw my works forty years. Wherefore I was grieved with that generation, and said, They do always err in their heart, and they have not known my ways. So I swore in my wrath, They shall not enter into my rest. Take heed, my brethren, lest there be in any of you an evil heart of unbelief, in departing from the living God. But exhort one another daily, while it is called Today, lest any of you be hardened through the deceitfulness of sin" (Heb.3:7–13). "For he saith, I have heard thee in a time accepted, and in the day of salvation have I helped thee: behold, now is the accepted time; behold, now is the day of salvation" (2 Cor.6:2).

"Tomorrow" is one of the devil's favorite words, but the truth is we don't know what will be on the next day. Another truth is that tomorrow turns into tomorrows in a heartbeat. Life goes by in a blur. If at this moment you sense the Holy Spirit calling you to repentance and salvation then respond in faith and receive Christ as your Savior and Lord. (See John 1:12). If you are born again and not living like it then humble yourself at the throne of grace, ask God for His mercy and grace to help you get where you should be. (See Heb. 4:16). Pride will make you a stranger at the throne of grace, but humility will make you a welcomed friend. If you hear His voice, don't delay another day.

If you wait until you find perfection in Christians before you come to Christ, you will never come; but if you are looking for perfection in a Savior, look no further. Don't delay another moment. Make all haste, come to Him now.

A Prayer of Blessing

Regardless of where you are in your journey of faith, I pray the Lord will guide you with wisdom from above, that He will protect you from all evil and the evil one. I pray He will bless your mind with an ability to think clearly on Biblical principles. I pray He will bless your emotions with stability and the genuine joy of the Lord. I pray He will give you a genuine hunger and thirst for the Word of God and prayer and that you become strengthened, established and settled in the faith. I pray He will provide for your physical needs of food, shelter and raiment. I pray the trails of life not overwhelm you and should a crisis come, you will not question His ultimate goodness and concern for your wellbeing. I pray He will provide you with godly friends that would enhance your walk with the Lord and not diminish it. I pray He will bless your home with the sweet fellowship of the Holy Spirit and that all who dwell there would grow in the grace and knowledge of the Lord Jesus Christ.

"The Lord bless thee, and keep thee; The Lord make his face shine upon thee, and be gracious unto thee; The Lord lift up his countenance upon thee, and give thee peace" (Num. 6:24–26).